Original title:

Finding Your Pod

Editor: Jessica Elisabeth Luik

Author: Kene Elistrand

ISBN HARDBACK: 978-9916-86-381-7

ISBN PAPERBACK: 978-9916-86-382-4

Celestial Streams

Stars whisper secrets in the night,
Guiding dreams with tender light.
The moon's soft glow on water beams,
Reflecting love in celestial streams.

Through twilight hues, their stories weave,
In constellations, who'd believe?
Their glow profound, a midnight serenade,
In heavenly waters, dreams cascade.

Silent rivers of the cosmic dance,
Drifting in an astral trance.
Eternity flows in silver gleams,
Within the endless, celestial streams.

Nautical Notes

Waves hum tunes of ocean deep,
Lullabies for those who sleep.
With every crest, a tale retold,
In nautical notes, secrets unfold.

Gulls' cries mix with the sailors' songs,
Melodies where the heart belongs.
O'er blue expanse, dreams gently float,
On the tender notes of a nautical boat.

The sea's vast choir sings with grace,
Echoes in the timeless space.
Harmony found in endless quotes,
Of life at sea, in nautical notes.

Echoes in Aquamarine

Beneath the waves, a world unseen,
Where echoes dance in aquamarine.
Whispers of the ocean's lore,
In liquid light, forevermore.

Coral gardens gently sway,
In rhythm with the ocean's play.
Voices of the deep convene,
In silent songs of aquamarine.

Dolphins' laughter, whales' great sigh,
In harmony beneath the sky.
Through the depths, our dreams careen,
On echoes soft in aquamarine.

Playful Ripples

Upon the lake, where breezes tease,
Ripples dance with playful ease.
Sunlight glints on waves that shimmer,
In joyous dance, they softly glimmer.

Laughter of the brook flows by,
Underneath a bright blue sky.
Nature's joy in gentle tripples,
Expressed in carefree, playful ripples.

Echoes of a whispered breeze,
Carried over tranquil seas.
Life's lighthearted, simple stipples,
Reflected in these playful ripples.

In Harbors and Hearts

Journeys start with whispered dreams,
Seaward paths where sunlight gleams.
Harbors hold the waiting tides,
Love and hope that never hides.

Vessels sail with hearts entwined,
A voyage beyond space and time.
In every port, a new embrace,
Anchored deep in love's sweet grace.

Storms may come and waters churn,
Lessons in the waves we learn.
Through the night, together stay,
Guiding stars that light our way.

Sightless Shorelines

Beyond the gaze of mortal eyes,
Lies a world that ever lies.
Sightless shorelines, secrets keep,
Ancient whispers, buried deep.

Waves that crash on hidden sands,
Echo tales from distant lands.
Veiled in mist, the ocean's breathe,
Silent stories of life and death.

Glimpse the truths within the haze,
Navigate the ceaseless maze.
Eyes may close, but souls will see,
Endless fields of mystery.

Fluid Families

Drifting in the ocean's fold,
We are threads in currents bold.
Families made in liquid bonds,
Sharing dreams of which they're fond.

Tides that bind us, ever strong,
Carry us where we belong.
In the dance of foam and wave,
Silent vows we always crave.

From one shore to distant isle,
We are kin in every mile.
Ocean's heart, our binding ties,
Fluid love beneath the skies.

Celestial Currents

Stars weave through the night,
On rivers of glowing light,
Waves in cosmic tides,
Galaxies dance in flight.

Moon whispers to the sea,
In silvery symphony,
Tides rise and fall in grace,
Reflections of infinity.

Planets carve their course,
In an orbital embrace,
Cosmic winds entwine,
In a timeless, gentle race.

Nebulae form in glow,
Breathing life, soft and slow,
In this vast expanse,
All of time starts to flow.

Comets blaze their trail,
Across the void so pale,
In the silent night,
Celestial stories hail.

Rhythms of Resonance

Feel the heartbeat of the earth,
In the whispering winds' mirth,
Drumming in the silent ground,
Where life's echoes are found.

In the forest, leaves will sway,
Singing in their ancient way,
Nature hums a soothing tune,
Underneath the silver moon.

Mountains mumble, rivers sing,
In a harmony they bring,
Each vibration tells a tale,
Where the world's wonders prevail.

Seas with rhythmic waves collide,
Oceans roar and then subside,
In their depths, a chorus thrives,
Every creature's voice survives.

In this symphony so grand,
We are notes in nature's band,
Rhythms of the earth resound,
In this resonance, we're found.

Drifters and Dreamers

Adrift in the sea of stars,
Wanderers without scars,
Dreamers sail in twilight's glow,
Chasing truths we barely know.

Across the night's expanse,
With dreams of happenstance,
We seek a fleeting glimpse,
Of cosmic significance.

Visions bloom in minds so free,
Boundless as the open sea,
Creation in the heart ignite,
In the quiet of the night.

Paths woven by dreams align,
To constellations so divine,
We drift on dreams' embrace,
To find our secret place.

Guided by the starry streams,
In the corridors of dreams,
Drifters find their way,
In cosmic ballet, they sway.

Harmony in the Deep

In the depths where silence lies,
Beneath the ocean's skies,
A world of wonders sleep,
Harmony in the deep.

Whales sing in low refrain,
Mysteries they explain,
In echoes long and vast,
Songs of the ocean's past.

Coral reefs in colors bright,
Dance with the moving light,
Fish in schools align,
In a ballet so divine.

Tides whisper ancient lore,
To the endless ocean floor,
In each wave, a melody,
Of life's endless symphony.

In this aquatic realm,
Nature at the helm,
A tranquil, silent sweep,
Harmony in the deep.

Tidal Trust

Upon the shore where dreams convene,
The ocean whispers secrets pure.
Waves carry tales of what's unseen,
A bond of faith forever sure.

In moonlit beams, the waters sigh,
Reflecting stars that twinkle bright.
Beneath their gaze, our hearts rely,
On tides that guide through darkest night.

With each caress, the shoreline bends,
Embracing all that life can send.
In ebb and flow, assurance lends,
A trust that time shall never end.

Within the depths, where shadows play,
A world of wonder lies below.
Together, through the storms we'll sway,
In tidal trust, our spirits grow.

Beneath Boundless Blue

Beneath the sky of azure hue,
We find our dreams and spirits soar.
With every breath, the world anew,
Infinite realms for us to explore.

The sun bestows its warming grace,
Golden threads in endless skies.
In open fields, we find our place,
Where freedom's call within us lies.

Clouds drift in patterns, soft and kind,
Stories written in the air.
In boundless blue, we seek and find,
A canvas vast, without compare.

Mountains rise and valleys dip,
Nature's wonders vast and true.
Together on this endless trip,
Beneath the boundless, brilliant blue.

Soul Migrations

Across the skies on wings of thought,
Our spirits journey far and wide.
In dreams, our souls are gently caught,
By winds that lift us, side by side.

Through realms unknown, we glide in peace,
Among the stars and cosmic streams.
Destinations without cease,
Guided by our inner dreams.

Each migration charts a tale,
Of love, of loss, of pure desire.
In every flight, we shall prevail,
Transcending life, ascending higher.

When dawn awakens us anew,
The journey doesn't seek an end.
For every soul that once withdrew,
Returns to life, begins to mend.

Ripple Resonance

In tranquil ponds where silence speaks,
A single drop ignites the scene.
Ripples dance in gentle creaks,
A resonance of thoughts serene.

From center midst, waves outward flow,
Touching shores with soft caress.
In quiet echoes, hearts shall know,
A sequence born of tenderness.

The surface glimmers, light and bright,
Reflecting skies, the sun's embrace.
In every ripple, pure delight,
A moment's peace, a touch of grace.

In waters still, where calm resides,
A deeper truth begins to sing.
That life, in circles, gently glides,
A harmony in everything.

Heartbeats in Harmony

In sync our pulses play,
A melody divine,
Through night and through day,
Our heartbeats intertwine.

With every breath we take,
A symphony so sweet,
As dreams begin to wake,
Our souls in rhythm meet.

Two hearts that beat as one,
Beneath the moonlit sky,
Until the morning sun,
We'll never say goodbye.

In love's pure harmony,
Eternal and so true,
Within this symphony,
Forever me and you.

Beyond the Horizon

Where sky and ocean kiss,
A world awaits unknown,
In dreams of endless bliss,
We wander all alone.

Horizons call our name,
With whispers soft and bright,
We'll chase the golden flame,
Through day and into night.

On wings of hope we fly,
Beyond the farthest shore,
Where secrets softly lie,
We'll find what we adore.

In lands of mystery,
Where endless wonders wait,
Together you and me,
We'll craft our destined fate.

Tides of Togetherness

The ebb and flow of time,
Waves washing on the shore,
In rhythms so sublime,
Our hearts embrace once more.

With every rising tide,
Our bond grows ever strong,
Through currents we will glide,
In love's eternal song.

The ocean's gentle sigh,
A lullaby so sweet,
Beneath the moonlit sky,
Together we'll retreat.

In unity, we stand,
As tides of life do guide,
Forever hand in hand,
We'll sail the ocean wide.

Beneath the Azure Sky

Beneath the azure sky,
Where dreams and wishes blend,
We'll let our spirits fly,
And on the breeze ascend.

Among the clouds so high,
Our hopes begin to soar,
With each breath we rely,
On love forevermore.

In fields of endless blue,
Our laughter fills the air,
A world meant just for two,
A perfect love we share.

As daylight starts to fade,
And stars light up the night,
In dreams we softly wade,
Our hearts forever bright.

The Search for Unity

Through tangled paths, we roam so far,
Beneath the same horizon's star,
With hopes and dreams, our guiding light,
In shadows, still, we seek the night.

From different lands and tongues we speak,
The common ground we come to seek,
In unity, our strength revealed,
Together, all our wounds are healed.

The barriers that once were strong,
Now crumble as we move along,
A tapestry of hearts entwined,
A clearer purpose, redefined.

In unity, we find our place,
Beyond the pain, beyond the race,
With hands upheld, we reach as one,
Our journey forward just begun.

Let peace and love become our creed,
In every thought and every deed,
For only then, we'll truly see,
The beauty of humanity.

Echoes of Belonging

In whispered winds, my soul does hear,
A call so distant, yet so near,
Among the voices soft and pure,
A sense of home that must endure.

Through valleys low and mountains high,
Beneath the vast, unending sky,
I seek the place where I belong,
In harmony, where hearts are strong.

The echoes of the past reside,
Within the depths I cannot hide,
A resonating, gentle tone,
A longing for a love unknown.

Within the crowd, alone I stand,
Yet feel the touch of another's hand,
A bond that's forged in silent grace,
A home within another's face.

Oh, let the echoes guide me true,
To spaces wide and ever new,
Where every heart can find its song,
In a world where we all belong.

Tribe of Kindred Souls

Amidst the wild and roaring tide,
We find a place where we confide,
In hearts alike and minds that glow,
A kinship deep within does grow.

Through trials dark and joys so bright,
Together we embrace the night,
In whispers shared and stories told,
A tribe of kindred souls unfolds.

No walls divide our tender ties,
For in each other, truth applies,
We walk as one with fearless hearts,
In unity, our journey starts.

The strength of many, forged as one,
Beneath the moon, beneath the sun,
A tribe that dances in the storm,
Together, we create the norm.

So, hand in hand, through time and space,
With love, we fill each empty place,
A family, by choice, we stand,
To face the world, as one, so grand.

Where Hearts Align

Where silence meets the evening breeze,
And longing hearts find sweet release,
In spaces where the stars align,
Two souls become a single sign.

Upon the pathway, undefined,
Through shadows dark and thoughts confined,
A spark ignites, a beam so bright,
In unity, we find our sight.

The wandering steps of yesteryears,
Now guided by a love that steers,
A journey shared by hearts entwined,
In moments where our paths combined.

With every breath, we breathe anew,
A covenant so deep and true,
Where dreams collide and hopes ignite,
In tender arms, we find the light.

So let our voyage cast away,
The fears, the doubts that once held sway,
For in this dance, our hearts define,
The sacred space where souls align.

Bonded by Harmony

In the quiet dawn light,
Hearts meld, calm and bright.
Whispers of the morning breeze,
Carry secrets with ease.

Voices blend in soft chorus,
Sharing stories, never porous.
Eyes meet in silent sync,
In harmony, spirits drink.

Hands clasped in gentle hold,
Against the day's rise, bold.
Steps align on shared paths,
In unity, love outlasts.

Laughter like a sweet refrain,
Eases every passing pain.
Moments weave a rich tapestry,
Bonded by harmony.

Silence speaks in tender chords,
Words become mere roads.
In togetherness, we find our song,
Burning bright, forever long.

Symphony of Kinship

Strings of fate intertwine,
In melodies, hearts define.
Tuned to love's grand design,
A symphony, pure and fine.

Notes of laughter, high and sweet,
In the rhythm, souls greet.
Through crescendos and falls,
Life's music forever calls.

Harmonies rich, friendships true,
In each chord, old bonds renew.
Touches light, yet resonate,
In kinship, hearts elevate.

Every verse a shared tale,
Every beat, soft or frail.
Through the quiet and the roar,
Together, we explore.

Symphony that time reveals,
Hearts as one, a wheel that heals.
In kinship, we find our song,
Symphony of love, lifelong.

Under the Same Moon

In the night's serene embrace,
We find a common place.
Miles apart, yet near,
Dreams shine crystal clear.

The moonlight's gentle kiss,
A silent, silvery bliss.
Guides our wandering minds,
To where our hearts find.

Stars whisper tales afar,
Of love's eternal bar.
Underneath the cosmic dance,
We belong, by chance.

Though shadows may intervene,
Faith in the unseen.
Bridges built on lunar glow,
Link where rivers flow.

United by the lunar gleam,
In nocturnal, whispered dream.
Under the same serene,
Our souls convene.

Echoes in the Waves

Whispers of the ocean's song,
In waves, we all belong.
Rhythm of the Earth's heart,
Tearing every doubt apart.

Crashing waves, a symphony,
Nature's timeless harmony.
In the lull of the sea,
Eternal bond is free.

Sands beneath the trodden foot,
Witness life's gentle root.
Echoes in the waves we see,
Reflections of you and me.

Tidal currents pull us near,
Carrying whispers dear.
In the ebb and flow of time,
Our spirits rhyme.

Breezes carry tales afar,
Through the ocean's reservoir.
Echoes in the waves we weave,
Life's legacy to retrieve.

Navigating by Stars

In a sea of midnight blue,
Constellations mark the way,
Guiding souls with gentle light,
Through the night until the day.

Dreams are mapped in ancient skies,
Velvet paths of twinkling charms,
Stories told by distant fires,
Cradled safe in starlit arms.

Whispers of celestial tales,
Echo in the silent night,
Silent guides to wayward hearts,
Leading them to morning's light.

Eyes shall trace the cosmic lines,
Seeking wisdom, seeking fate,
Navigating doubts and fears,
To horizons, wide and great.

As the dawn begins to break,
Stars retreat from amber skies,
But their wisdom lingers on,
In our hearts and in our eyes.

Fluid Friendships

Like a river flowing free,
Friendships twist and turn and bend,
Moving through both gentle streams,
And the rapids, at the end.

Waters blend in quiet pools,
Where the heart finds calm and rest,
Flowing over rocks and roots,
Smoothing edges by their quest.

In the current, trust is built,
Carving paths through days and years,
Shaping lives, as rivers do,
Washing away doubts and fears.

Tide and time, they ebb and flow,
Never constant, always change,
Yet the bonds remain unbroken,
In a world that's rearranged.

Friends are like the waters free,
Adapting to the paths they find,
In the flow of fleeting time,
Ever present, intertwined.

Beneath the Surface

Beneath the surface, shadows play,
Secrets hidden, deep and dark,
In the quiet, murky depths,
Lies the soul's forgotten spark.

Whispers float through liquid nights,
Mysteries of the cold abyss,
In the stillness, life persists,
Silent, unseen, yet amiss.

Truths are veiled in layers deep,
Masked by ripples on the top,
Only those who dare to dive,
See where dreams begin and stop.

Searching through the silent seas,
Echoes of a distant call,
Hoping for the light below,
To illuminate it all.

Surface breaks to breaths anew,
Emerging from the hidden wold,
Revelations, raw and true,
Waiting for the brave and bold.

The Dance of Kindred Spirits

In the quiet, sacred spaces,
Where the heart meets kindred soul,
There begins a subtle rhythm,
Silent dance to make us whole.

Steps are traced in harmony,
With a love both fresh and old,
Grace and joy in every motion,
Stories of the dance retold.

Eyes that shimmer, hands that touch,
In the dance of life's embrace,
Moments blend in sweet surrender,
Closer drawn with every pace.

Through the ups and downturns spinning,
Trust is built in every twirl,
With each step, the bond is growing,
Ever strong in our small world.

In the waltz of kindred spirits,
Bound by ties both deep and true,
We find peace and deeper meaning,
In the dance of me and you.

The Confluence of Spirits

In the echo of dreams where shadows blend,
A dance of souls begins and never ends.
Whispers of ancient tales in twilight's glow,
Merge in the river's undulating flow.

Colors of dusk weave through the air,
Uniting spirits free from worldly care.
Together they swirl in a cosmic flight,
Bound by the moon's gentle, guiding light.

Through the night, they chase the dawn,
Yearning for a day that's yet unborn.
Their essence mingles as soft winds sing,
Creatures of the cosmos, eternal spring.

Paths intertwine where boundaries cease,
In moments of silence, profound peace.
A symphony of lives, blending as one,
Journey's end just begun.

In this merging, freedom's found,
A circle where no edges are bound.
Together they rise on wings anew,
Spirits conjoined in ethereal dew.

Seeking Our Symbiosis

Together in this woven thread,
A tapestry of lives widespread.
Interlaced, our destinies lie,
Beneath an endless, star-strewn sky.

Through whispered winds and flowing streams,
We share our hopes, our fears, our dreams.
Seeking balance in the sway,
Of night and day, rise and decay.

In nature's breath, in every sigh,
An unspoken pact, you and I.
Bound by soil, by air, by sea,
Seeking harmony in unity.

Roots entwined beneath the earth,
A silent promise since our birth.
In symbiosis, we find grace,
In each other's silent embrace.

Together we bloom, together we fade,
A cycle of life in balance laid.
Hand in hand, we walk this path,
A symbiotic aftermath.

The Path to Our Tribe

Through the woods where shadows play,
We seek our tribe along the way.
Heartbeats guide us in the night,
Toward a fire's beckoning light.

Echoes of laughter fill the air,
Stories told with loving care.
Hand in hand, we traverse time,
In rhythm with an ancient chime.

Steps in sync, our spirits rise,
Underneath the boundless skies.
In unity, we find our strength,
A bond that stretches time and length.

From dawn's glow to twilight's end,
With every curve and every bend.
Our quest for belonging never tires,
Walking paths where love inspires.

Connected hearts, a gathered band,
Spread across this sacred land.
Together we forge, together we strive,
Walking the path to find our tribe.

Unified Currents

In the sea of life's vast embrace,
Currents intertwine, leaving no trace.
Each ripple, a story, quietly told,
In waters both warm and cold.

We flow together, side by side,
In this ocean, vast and wide.
Embracing waves, we rise and fall,
Unified in nature's call.

The depths conceal ancient lore,
Tales of those who swam before.
In their wake, we find our way,
Through tempest, calm, night, and day.

Our pulses sync with tidal breath,
In this dance of life and death.
A seamless web of threads so fine,
Interwoven, yours and mine.

Together we chart the boundless blue,
Unified currents, me and you.
In harmony, we'll always be,
Bound by the spirit of the sea.

Bridges to Brotherhood

Across the river deep and wide,
We built a bridge with beams of pride,
Strangers once, now hand in hand,
Together we forge, united we stand.

Through storms and waves, our path was fraught,
But friendship is the treasure sought,
Strong and true, the bond grows tight,
Illuminating our darkest night.

In every laugh and every cheer,
In whispered dreams that we hold dear,
We find our strength, our common scope,
In brotherhood, our endless hope.

The currents rage, the winds may blow,
Yet through it all, this love will grow,
For every step across this span,
Is a testament to our grand plan.

So let us walk, both side by side,
With faith and honor, as our guide,
Bridges to brotherhood we've paved,
Together free, together saved.

The Embrace of Our Clan

In the circle of our clan so dear,
We share our joys, and quell our fear,
With arms open wide, hearts in tune,
Basking beneath the same bright moon.

Each story told, each lesson shared,
In this embrace, we've always cared,
Generations blend, old and new,
A legacy rich, a love so true.

Hands that once were small and weak,
Now lend support, when words can't speak,
In laughter's echo, in music's flow,
The essence of our kin does show.

Through trials faced and victories won,
Standing together, we become one,
The bond unbroken, ever tight,
A beacon in the darkest night.

In every heart, this truth does stand,
The strength within The Embrace of Our Clan,
Bound by love, by fate and choice,
Together we rise, in unity, rejoice.

Whispers in the Crowd

Among the throngs, in cities vast,
Whispers carry, slow and fast,
Secrets shared in fleeting glance,
Moments caught in a silent dance.

Eyes that meet, then swiftly part,
Still leave an imprint on the heart,
In whispers soft, the stories flow,
Anonymity we can't outgrow.

In crowded streets and busy lanes,
In whispered hopes and quiet pains,
Connections form, then fade away,
Yet mark the soul in subtle ways.

Voices merge in a muted hum,
Where we all speak, yet feel so numb,
In the crowd, we seek out peace,
A sense of calm, a sweet release.

So listen close, with open ears,
Through whispers, conquer all your fears,
In the noise, find what is true,
A whisper might just be for you.

Circle of Resonance

In a space where echoes blend,
Harmony and tension mend,
We find the flow, the endless link,
Where hearts align and spirits sink.

Vibrations hum, and we unite,
In a circle, pure and bright,
Each word spoken, each note played,
In Circle of Resonance, we've laid.

In every pulse, in every beat,
Connection's found where souls meet,
The rhythm guides, the cadence draws,
Transcending time, adhering laws.

Hands entwined in perfect grace,
Finding virtue, finding place,
In every touch, and every sound,
A unity profound is found.

So let us join, with hearts as one,
In circles where life's threads are spun,
In resonance, our spirits bound,
In this Circle, we're forever found.

The Pilot Star's Guide

Through the night so clear and bright,
The pilot star takes its flight.
Guiding sailors toward their dreams,
Across the seas where moonlight gleams.

Maps unravel, stars align,
In the celestial design.
Voyages taken hand in hand,
By the pilot star's command.

Shadows dance with whispered grace,
In the ancient, timeless space.
The horizon calls with gentle might,
Underneath the starry light.

Wisdom passed from night to day,
In the skies where legends lay.
Trust the guide through calm and storm,
Where the pilot star is warm.

Charting the Vast Blue

On horizons vast and wide,
Mysteries of the ocean hide.
Every wave a tale untold,
In the deep blue story old.

Mast and sail against the sky,
Where the seabirds swift do fly.
Charting paths in waters cold,
With the stars as guides of old.

Compass turns with steady grace,
Guiding to each hidden place.
Where the currents swift and true,
Chart the course in endless blue.

Every ripple speaks a name,
In the voyage's eternal fame.
Navigators brave and few,
Charting worlds in boundless blue.

Echoes of the Deep

Beneath the waves where silence reigns,
Lies a world of hidden gains.
Creatures swim in shadows dark,
In the deep where whispers hark.

Ancient echoes softly sound,
In the depths where secrets are found.
Coral gardens, forests tall,
Echoes of the ocean's call.

Sunlight fades to twilight glow,
In the waters down below.
Songs of whales through currents drift,
In the deep where shadows shift.

Legends told in bubbles rise,
Mysteries beneath the skies.
In the deep where echoes keep,
Secrets in the ocean's sleep.

Silent Signals

In the stillness of the night,
Silent signals, soft and light.
Whispers travel on the breeze,
Through the rustling of the trees.

Lightning's flash, a distant star,
Tales of times both near and far.
Silent signals gently seam,
Reality with wistful dreams.

Echoes of the heart's own tune,
Played beneath the watchful moon.
Messages in shadows cast,
In the silent, quiet vast.

Eyes that see and hearts that feel,
Know the silence is surreal.
Signals whispered in the dark,
Leave a resonating mark.

By Ebb and Flow

The waves, they kiss the shore with grace,
Then pull away, leaving a trace,
A dance of tides, in nature's rhyme,
Marking passage of fleeting time.

Gulls cry out, a chorus free,
As salt and wind shape destiny,
Each grain of sand a tale to tell,
Of where it landed, how it fell.

The moon, a lantern in the sky,
Commands the water, low and high,
In constant motion, to and fro,
Lives are shaped by ebb and flow.

Seaweed sways in tandem, free,
Embracing waves' sheer potency,
Their supple dance, a liquid art,
In tide and current, love impart.

Thrum of ocean, deep and vast,
Echoes of the ages past,
In every crest and every trough,
We find our place, though oh so soft.

Sailing with Spirits

Whispers ride on salted breeze,
Carrying myths down through the seas,
Ancient mariners' ghostly calls,
Through moonlit nights and tempests' squalls.

Canvas stretched, the sails ignite,
With tales of valiant, daring flight,
Every creak of weathered wood,
Tells stories long misunderstood.

Mermaids sing their haunting tune,
To silver light of crescent moon,
Selkies dance in twilight's glow,
Where spectral tides and spirits flow.

Compass fixed to starlit guide,
Where sea and sky and souls collide,
In every gust, a whispered name,
Of sailors lost to fortune's game.

Beyond horizon, dreams await,
In hands of spirits, gentle fate,
Set sail with hope in hearts agleam,
Across the ocean's boundless dream.

Oceanic Embrace

In twilight's glow, the sea unfolds,
A whisper soft, a story told,
Of depths unknown and mysteries steep,
Where secrets of the ocean sleep.

The waves like lovers' arms extend,
In tender curves they rise, they bend,
Inviting hearts to beat in time,
With rhythmic pulse, so pure, sublime.

Beneath the surface, worlds unseen,
Coral castles bathed in green,
Life abounds in silent show,
Beneath the moon's soft, tender glow.

Currents waltz in fluid grace,
Every movement, a warm embrace,
Embodying the world's ancient song,
In ocean's depths, we all belong.

Sky and sea merge at the edge,
Where dreams and hopes in whispers pledge,
A unity, forever bound,
In ocean's love, our peace is found.

Blue Horizon's Found

Morning mist, it lifts away,
Revealing dawn's first blushing ray,
Horizon whispers, blue and vast,
An open book of futures cast.

Skies stretch wide in azure sweep,
Where seagulls chase the sun's first peep,
A promise of the day ahead,
In sky and sea, our spirits wed.

Each breath of air feels crisp and new,
As waves unveil their endless hue,
A dance of light on liquid blue,
A world bathed in celestial view.

Boundless dreams on distant line,
Where mortal and eternal twine,
Hope sails on that endless plane,
In quest for joy, through calm and rain.

Let hearts set course for faraway,
And follow where the horizons play,
In every wake and starry end,
Blue horizon's call, our faithful friend.

Anchors in the Abyss

Beneath the waters, deep and cold,
Where secrets of the ocean hold,
We find our anchors, golden, bold,
In stories of the seas retold.

These chains that bind us to the past,
Through tempests fierce, they hold us fast,
Each link a memory built to last,
In waters still, or stormy blast.

In shadows where the sunlight fades,
And twilight hushes final raids,
Our anchors, firm, in dark cascades,
In depth and darkness, strength parades.

When hope seems lost to endless blue,
Anchors whisper, old and true,
That in the deep, where dreams pursue,
Lies the courage born anew.

Anchors resting, silent might,
In the abyss, where stars alight,
Guide our hearts through endless night,
To morning dawn—a beacon's sight.

Waters of Whimsy

In waters wild, the dolphins play,
They leap and dance, in light array,
Through waves they chase the bright bouquet,
Of bubbles bursting in display.

The fishes laugh as currents spin,
With tails that twirl beneath the fin,
They swirl with sounds of violin,
In waters whispering with a grin.

The turtles glide in waltz serene,
Through emerald depths, in places unseen,
Their movements paint a tranquil scene,
Where whimsy reigns, a submarine.

The jellyfish with tentacles bright,
Glow gently through the moonlit night,
Their dances weave a web of light,
In waters dreaming limitless flight.

Oh, waters of whimsy, wild and free,
A realm of mirth and mystery,
You hold within your heart the key,
To boundless joy and fantasy.

Unity in the Depths

Beneath the waves, where silence sings,
A tale of unity deep it brings,
Of creatures small with mighty wings,
Together bound by ocean strings.

The coral whispers secrets old,
Of unity in hearts so bold,
In every hue and shade, it's told,
In depths where all life's dreams unfold.

The schools of fish in colors bright,
Move as one through darkest night,
In synchronized and flawless flight,
They show their strength in shared delight.

The whales' songs through waters hum,
A symphony to which they come,
From distant shores they gather, sum,
In unity, they beat the drum.

In ocean's depths, the hearts entwine,
In currents' pulse, a sacred sign,
A bond that through the tides will shine,
Eternal, deep, and so divine.

Waves of Companionship

Amidst the tides where stories flow,
In waves that come and waves that go,
Companionship begins to grow,
In bonds that only oceans know.

Each wave a whisper, soft and true,
Of friendships born in waters blue,
With every crest, a pledge anew,
In depths unseen to eyes in view.

The shells that gather on the shore,
Each bears a tale of bond and lore,
Of journeys shared forevermore,
In waves that echo friendship's core.

The sands embrace beneath our feet,
A place where hearts in rhythm beat,
In union where the waters meet,
Companionship so pure and sweet.

Oh, waves of friendship, timeless tide,
Together through the storm we ride,
In you, our hearts are opened wide,
And in your arms, our souls abide.

Harbor of Hope

In the dawn of warming light,
Anchors lift from depths below,
Dreams set sail, new and bright,
In this harbor, hope will grow.

Waves of courage, whispers near,
Guiding hearts toward skies so wide,
In this refuge, free from fear,
The future flows with faithful tide.

Stars above in vigil staid,
Light the path for those who stray,
Haven where no light shall fade,
Here, our spirits find their way.

Through the tempest, through the storm,
Harbor still, a steadfast guide,
Cradle hearts, keep them warm,
In your shelter, we confide.

Glorious dawn will greet the morn,
Harbor where new hopes are born,
From this embrace, never torn,
Life anew, by light adorned.

Blue Haven

Upon the azure's gentle grace,
Dreams like waves in tender dance,
Safe within this tranquil place,
We hold onto every chance.

Seas of blue, where wishes sway,
Skies that merge with ocean's line,
Here the restless find their way,
In this haven, all is fine.

Every tear the tide erases,
Every sorrow washed away,
In this refuge, love embraces,
Peace like shells on sand shall lay.

Hearts aligned with ocean's song,
Whispered hopes to stars we give,
In this blue, where we belong,
Bound by dreams, in time, we live.

Endless sky and boundless sea,
In this haven, souls set free,
Lost in blue, eternally,
Love and peace, our destiny.

Surface Smiles

Masks we wear with practiced grace,
Surface smiles, a gentle guise,
Veiling truths no one can trace,
Hiding souls behind our eyes.

Laughing light in shadows play,
Mirrored tales of fleeting glee,
Beneath the surface, hearts betray,
Secrets longing to break free.

Silken words we weave in jest,
Curtains drawn before our minds,
In the depths, our selves suppressed,
Yearning for what solace finds.

Whispers held by unseen chains,
Surface smiles mask the pains,
In this dance of silent strains,
Faith and hope are what remains.

Truth will dawn and lights will shine,
Surface smiles will fall away,
Unveil the heart's truest line,
In pure love, no mask shall stay.

Soulwaves

In the ebb and flow of night,
Soulwaves crash on dreams' far shore,
Carrying whispers, soft and light,
Echoes of what's come before.

Waves of memory, tides of time,
Currents deep within us lie,
In each crest, a silent rhyme,
As our spirits reach the sky.

Oceans vast within us stir,
Every heartbeat, every sigh,
In the soul's deep, dreams confer,
Woven thoughts that cannot die.

Flowing into endless day,
Soulwaves bear our hopes along,
Guiding us upon our way,
To where the spirit's light is strong.

Boundless depths of heart and mind,
In these waves, true self we find,
Soulwaves endless, undefined,
In their motion, love's enshrined.

Songs of the Sea

Waves crash upon the lonely shore,
Their whispers held in ageless lore.
The seagulls dance in sky so free,
Eternal songs of the sea.

Moonlit tides and midnight sails,
Weaving through the starry trails.
Siren's call in winds so strong,
A timeless, haunting ocean song.

Sunrise paints the horizon deep,
Awakens dreams from silent sleep.
Fishermen cast their nets so wide,
Hopes and wishes, the ocean's tide.

Ships embark on paths unknown,
Guided by stars, the sea their throne.
In every wave, a secret keeps,
The songs of the sea in hearts it weeps.

Rocky cliffs meet ocean's embrace,
Nature's symphony leaves a trace.
In every shell, a story lies,
The songs of the sea, beneath the skies.

A Symphony of Souls

In twilight's glow, the world unfolds,
A symphony of souls untold.
Whispers carried by the breeze,
Songs of life through ancient trees.

Every heartbeat finds a rhyme,
In the dance of space and time.
Souls converge in silent night,
Creating melodies of light.

Through valleys deep and mountains high,
Each spirit takes its chance to fly.
Echoes in the canyons wide,
A symphony where dreams reside.

Stars align in cosmic grace,
Reflecting in each soulful face.
Harmony in varied forms,
Through life's tempests, calms, and storms.

Together swaying, hand in hand,
Soulful notes across the land.
In every voice, a story rolls,
In this grand symphony of souls.

In the Realm of Dolphins

Beneath the waves, a world unseen,
Where dolphins play in turquoise sheen.
Their laughter echoes through the blue,
In realms where dreams and wonders grew.

Fluid grace through waters glide,
In harmony with ocean's tide.
Leaping arches touch the sky,
In realms of dolphins, spirits fly.

Ancient wisdom in their eyes,
A mystic force that never dies.
Communing in a silent speech,
Their language far beyond our reach.

Each ripple tells a tale of old,
Of mysteries and treasures bold.
Guides to realms where few have tread,
In oceans vast, their stories spread.

In twilight waters, silver gleam,
Dolphins guide us through the dream.
A world of magic, wild and free,
In the realm of dolphins, come and see.

The Call of Belonging

In quiet moments, whispers come,
A call that makes the heartbeats drum.
Through forest trails and city streets,
The call of belonging always meets.

In eyes of strangers, kind and warm,
In gentle hands that calm the storm.
A sense of place, a rhythm strong,
The call of belonging, a soulful song.

Home can be the open sky,
Or laughter shared as moments fly.
In words and actions, subtle signs,
We find the threads of fate's designs.

The echoes of our past entwine,
With hopes and dreams that brightly shine.
In every step, in every choice,
The call of belonging gives us voice.

So listen close, with open heart,
To the symphony of which we're part.
In every beat, in every song,
The call of belonging makes us strong.

Symphony of Companionship

In the quiet of dawn, we find solace,
Hand in hand, a world to embrace.
Every heartache, every joy revealed,
In this bond, our fates are sealed.

Through stormy nights and golden days,
Together we walk in varied ways.
In laughter's echo, in sorrow's sigh,
A friendship reaches beyond the sky.

On paths untrodden, yet side by side,
With trust our only guide.
In silence, or midst loud acclaim,
Our symphony forever the same.

Building dreams upon shared sands,
Connected through life's gentle hands.
No rift too grand, no tale untold,
In this companionship, we grow bold.

With every heartbeat, every breath,
We cherish this journey, defying death.
An endless symphony, so sweet and pure,
In each other, we find our cure.

Quest for Kinship

In the vast expanse of life's grand stage,
A wanderer seeks a golden age.
Through deserts barren, valleys green,
Kinship sought, yet never seen.

Whispers of hope on the wind do ride,
A spark in hearts where dreams abide.
With every step, a call so near,
A quest for kinship, strong and clear.

Mountains tall and rivers wide,
Bind the soul, yet can't divide.
In each shadow, a promise kept,
In each challenge, our bond is wept.

Threads of fate by hands unseen,
Weave a tapestry serene.
In kindred spirits, solace found,
A bond unbroken, profound.

Past horizons where the sun sets low,
Our kinship brightens with a glow.
In unity and love, our path aligned,
A quest fulfilled, forever twined.

Whispers of Unity

In whispers soft, unity speaks,
Through hearts that seek, the world it tweaks.
Together in strength, we rise anew,
In bonds of gold, our spirits grew.

Across divides, our voices merge,
In a quiet, relentless surge.
Hand in hand, through night and day,
In unity, we find our way.

Shadows fall, yet lights endure,
In unity, a love so pure.
Bound by dreams and aspirations,
Beyond life's many machinations.

Each whisper a note in harmony,
A symphony of destiny.
In every challenge, every stride,
Together we face the rising tide.

With hearts and minds forever keen,
In peace and war, and in between.
Whispers of unity, strong and true,
In every moment, our strength renew.

Seeker of Solace

In the quietude of night and day,
A seeker of solace finds his way.
Through the turmoil, through the pain,
Seeking peace in the falling rain.

Eyes that wander, hearts that yearn,
For a place where fires burn.
A warm embrace, a gentle touch,
In solace, they seek so much.

Footprints left on paths unknown,
In solitude, they find a home.
Listening to the winds that guide,
Finding solace by their side.

Soft whispers, gentle sighs,
A comfort beneath the starry skies.
In dreams, in hopes, a serene quest,
For solace, they never rest.

Through life's waves and calmest seas,
A seeker of solace finds their ease.
In each breath, a quiet claim,
In solace, they stake their name.

Journey to Our Circle

We walk the path of every dawn,
Where shadows play and dreams are drawn.
With every step, the world unfolds,
In stories new and legends old.

Through forests deep and deserts wide,
In storm and sun, we side by side.
With hearts as guides, our truth we find,
As stars ignite the endless mind.

Oceans whisper secrets vast,
Mountains echo voices past.
Hand in hand, we chase the song,
That binds our souls, where we belong.

Rivers flow with tales untold,
Of bonds that neither break nor fold.
In laughter, tears, and silent nights,
We weave our fates in shared delights.

Circle strong with love and trust,
Built not in gold but simple dust.
With every soul, the journey grows,
In unity, our circle knows.

Harmony's Quest

In fields of green, beneath the sky,
We seek the notes that never die.
A symphony of hearts and dreams,
Where every voice in chorus beams.

Through troubled seas and winds that moan,
Our spirits blend, yet stand alone.
Each melody, a thread of light,
In tapestry of endless night.

The mountains hum in ancient tone,
A rhythm carved in timeless stone.
We dance our hopes in vibrant hues,
In harmony that life imbues.

Across the stars, a silent plea,
To find the chord of unity.
With hands that reach and hearts that yearn,
We chase the song for which we burn.

So let us walk this winding quest,
In harmony, our spirits blessed.
For in each heart, a note does lie,
That makes the music never die.

The Call of Togetherness

In crowded halls and open fields,
The call to join, a force that heals.
With every bond, a string we weave,
A fabric strong with love we breathe.

Through whispered winds of silent night,
We journey forth, hearts burning bright.
In shared embrace, our spirits soar,
Together bound forevermore.

Beneath the moon's soft silver gleam,
We find the pulse, the common dream.
With every step and every glance,
We build a fate, a sacred dance.

Oceans wide and skies so blue,
Cannot contain our boundless view.
For in each soul, the call does ring,
A song of unity we sing.

So let us heed this timeless call,
Where hearts entwine and barriers fall.
In togetherness, we find our way,
A brighter dawn, a better day.

In the Arms of Allies

When skies are gray and storms arise,
We find our strength in friendly ties.
In moments dark, in times of need,
We lift each other, hearts that bleed.

Through battles fought and trials faced,
In allies' arms, our fears erased.
Their voices calm, their hands are sure,
Together strong, we shall endure.

Across the fields of doubt and pain,
With allies true, we break the chain.
In every tear, a story shared,
Of courage found, of spirits bared.

With laughter bright and whispers kind,
We heal the wounds, leave scars behind.
For in the arms of those we trust,
We rise anew, as stardust must.

So let us cherish every friend,
For in their hearts, our fears shall end.
In arms of allies, love we find,
A testament to humankind.

A Beacon of Brotherhood

In the darkest of nights, a light will shine,
A beacon of hope, so pure, divine.
Where hands reach out, hearts intertwine,
To lift each other, time after time.

With every step, together we tread,
On paths of joy and tears we've shed.
Bound by trust, no words unsaid,
In brotherhood's embrace, we're led.

Eyes that see in kindred dreams,
Souls that sail on shared streams.
In unity, strength beams,
A brotherhood, like sunlight, gleams.

Through storms of life, unbowed we stand,
In courage, love, hand in hand.
Led by a power, so grand,
Together we rise, a noble band.

Beneath the stars, we find our way,
In brotherhood, where hopes lay.
Bound by bonds that forever stay,
In each other's hearts, come what may.

Connection's Journey

Across the miles, our spirits roam,
In letters sent, in calls to home.
We bridge the gaps, no more alone,
A connection's journey, our hearts have known.

In laughter shared, in tears we've cried,
In moments where our souls abide.
We find the strength, side by side,
In connection's journey, we take pride.

Through winding roads and endless skies,
In gazes, smiles, our spirits rise.
In every farewell, in every sigh,
A connection's journey, never dies.

With every dawn, with every dusk,
In whispers soft, in bonds of trust.
In memories kept, our souls entrust,
A connection's journey, meant for us.

In paths we've crossed, in dreams we've spun,
In every race, in battles won.
Together we stand, as one begun,
A connection's journey, forever one.

Kinship's Odyssey

In seas of time, we set our sail,
On kinship's boat, we tell our tale.
Through tempests fierce, and winds that wail,
Together, we prevail.

In laughter's breeze, in sorrow's sea,
In moments where we simply be.
We chart our course, wild and free,
Kinship's odyssey, you and me.

Through waves of change, we drift and flow,
In currents deep, where dreams do grow.
With every tide, new paths we know,
Kinship's odyssey, we show.

In night and day, our journey winds,
In every heart, our story finds.
In rhythmic beat, our love entwines,
Kinship's odyssey, defines.

As stars above, our guide, our light,
In darkness, hope remains in sight.
Bound by kin, our spirits knight,
In kinship's odyssey, we unite.

Roots of Togetherness

Beneath the soil, our roots entwine,
In fields of hope, our hearts align.
Through time and change, a love divine,
In roots of togetherness, we find.

In every leaf, in every bloom,
In whispers soft, in night's calm gloom.
We grow as one, in nature's womb,
Together, we resume.

In rains that fall, in sun that gleams,
In waking hours, in silent dreams.
Our bond is strong, as mountain streams,
Togetherness, it seems.

With every season, passing by,
In colored leaves, in clear blue sky.
Our roots grow deep, we amplify,
Togetherness, we amplify.

In forest dense, or garden neat,
In every place, in every beat.
Our roots of love, pure and sweet,
Togetherness, complete.

The Fellowship We Crave

In the twilight, where shadows wane,
A bond unseen, yet felt profound.
Hearts converge and no longer feign,
In laughter's echo, joy is found.

Dwelling in the warmth of shared delight,
Threads weave thick in night and day.
Through every wrong and every right,
Together we navigate our way.

Whispers soft in twilight's glow,
Comfort in places no words can reach.
A friend to share all we know,
In silence, love finds its speech.

Upon this path that binds so tight,
Lanterns of hope, seem to guide.
In the presence of our light,
All sorrow and fears subside.

With every step, a heart feels free,
Courage drawn from hands we clasp.
In fellowship, it's clear to see,
We are more than shadows in life's grasp.

Gentle Bonding

Soft whispers of a sweet embrace,
Words unspoken, hearts aligned.
In every look, a tender trace,
Of stories shared, and love refined.

A gentle touch, a knowing gaze,
Bridges built that none can sever.
Through life's many capricious ways,
Our souls entwine, forever.

In quiet moments, deep and true,
This gentle bond grows ever strong.
In silence, we begin anew,
Two hearts in sync, where we belong.

Beyond the realms of time and space,
This gentle bond, it keeps us whole.
In every smile, a warm embrace,
Echoes sound within our soul.

Together, in this dance of life,
We find our peace, our souls refreshed.
Through gentle bonding, away from strife,
Our hearts, forever, intermeshed.

The Voyage of Commonality

Set sail on seas of shared desire,
With compass true, and hearts of fire.
Where waves of life cannot conspire,
To break the bonds that never tire.

Onward in our common quest,
With winds of unity to send.
In every trial, we're truly blessed,
In shoulders strong, and hearts to lend.

Charting maps of memory's shores,
The currents guide our kindred souls.
In every port, a friendship soars,
As truth and warmth our journey tolls.

Through storm and calm, we navigate,
With stars of hope above so bright.
Together we will celebrate,
The bonds that guide us through the night.

The voyage, endless, never known,
In commonality, we find our way.
For what is sown, our hearts have grown,
A brotherhood that none can sway.

Nest of Kindred Spirits

In a nest of kindred dreams,
Where souls collide in restful sigh.
We weave our hopes through sunlit beams,
And lift our voices to the sky.

Each branch, a memory cherished dear,
Each leaf, a promise held so tight.
In this cocoon, there's naught to fear,
For here, we find our purest light.

Whispers float on gentle breeze,
As laughter fills the morning air.
In simple moments such as these,
We find a heaven everywhere.

No storm can shake our sacred space,
No wind can sever what we've spun.
For in this nest, our hearts find grace,
And join as one beneath the sun.

Together, in this place of rest,
We share, we love, we comprehend.
In the nest of kindred, we are blessed,
With spirits bound until the end.

Journey to Our Nest

We wandered through the paths unknown,
With dreams and whispers softly sown.
The wind a guide, the stars aglow,
In twilight's hush, our spirits grow.

Together, arm in arm, we tread,
Through forests deep and skies of red.
Each step a promise, every mile,
Our hearts aligned, our souls compile.

Mountains high and rivers wide,
We scale them all, with hearts as guide.
A journey carved through space and time,
In sync, we dance, a love sublime.

The nights are cold, but we are warm,
In this cocoon, safe from the storm.
We build our nest with tender care,
A refuge strong beyond compare.

Through valleys green and deserts dry,
Our love a beacon in the sky.
We've reached the place where dreams invest,
Together now, we've found our nest.

The Odyssey of Friendship

Through seasons past and days to come,
Our bond is grown, a beating drum.
In laughter's echo, tears the same,
In friendship's heart, we write our name.

Across the seas, through storms we sail,
In every joy, we've shared the tale.
Through every trial, each life's test,
Our friendship proves it's truly blessed.

With hands entwined, we face the world,
Our banners high, unfurled, uncurled.
Together strong, we chart the course,
A friendship pure, a boundless force.

In darkest nights and brightest days,
Our paths align in myriad ways.
No storm too fierce, no mountain tall,
In unity, we conquer all.

Through every chapter, life has penned,
We'll stand together, friend with friend.
The odyssey of hearts entwined,
In friendship's light, we ever find.

In Sync with Souls

In silent whispers, hearts align,
Through space and time, a love divine.
With every beat, our spirits fuse,
In sync, our souls, their dance amuse.

The moon above, the earth below,
In this embrace, our feelings grow.
The stars bear witness to our grace,
Two souls in sync, in love's embrace.

With eyes that speak in silent cries,
We find our truth, no need for lies.
Our worlds collide, yet find their peace,
In sync, our hearts, their throb increase.

In moments fleeting, time stands still,
Our spirits blend, our dreams fulfill.
In every glance, in every sigh,
Together now, we touch the sky.

Through life's vast ocean, side by side,
We journey forth, our hearts as guide.
In sync with souls, we've found our whole,
A love complete, two kindred souls.

Kindred Paths Converge

Two roads once curved through forest deep,
In solitude, their echoes weep.
But fate's kind hand, a gentle urge,
And soon two kindred paths converge.

Through fields of gold and meadows green,
Where dreams and hopes are softly seen.
In harmony, our steps align,
A journey shared, with light divine.

The world around may twist and turn,
But in our hearts, a fire will burn.
In every trial, through joy and pain,
Together now, in love's refrain.

In every dawn, a promise new,
In every dusk, a sky of blue.
Our paths, entwined, in fate's dear weave,
In unity, we dare believe.

For kindred spirits, joined as one,
Through life's vast tapestry, we've spun.
In love divine, our hearts immerse,
Together now, our paths converge.

Oceans Apart

Waves crash upon distant shores,
With voices whispering so far.
In silence, your heart implores,
To bridge the distance, close the scar.

Beneath the moon's tender glow,
Our souls seem less estranged.
Seas may ebb, tides may flow,
Our love remains unchanged.

Stars guide sailors through the night,
As dreams traverse the dark seas.
Though separated by the light,
In love, we find our ease.

Each ripple holds a hopeful gleam,
Each gust a whispered prayer.
Oceans part, but in a dream,
Our spirits hover there.

Distances may stretch and sway,
Time may test and bend our way.
Yet through it all, we shall stay,
United 'cross the ocean's spray.

Hearts United

In the quiet of the dawn,
When the world is still asleep,
Two hearts bind and carry on,
In love, their secrets keep.

Like twin flames in serene night,
They dance and intertwine.
In every shadow, every light,
Their love's design aligns.

Moments shared are treasures grand,
Time cannot erase.
Side by side, hand in hand,
Together they embrace.

Through each trial, each event,
They find their strength anew.
Every challenge circumvent,
Their unity holds true.

In the story of their days,
Chapters filled with grace.
Hearts united, love portrays,
A bond no force can chase.

Marine Melodies

Whispers in the rolling tide,
Echoes of a seafarer's song.
In the depths where secrets hide,
Melodies gentle, strong.

Shells hum with the ocean's beat,
Coral choirs soft and bright.
Waves compose a rhythmic suite,
In the stillness of the night.

Dolphins leap with joyful grace,
Their calls a joyous sound.
Marine songs leave a trace,
On the waters all around.

Below, the whales call out in tune,
A symphony so grand.
Underneath the silver moon,
Voices weave across the sand.

Every note a tale unfolds,
Of mysteries and lore.
Marine melodies hold,
Songs that last forevermore.

Connected Currents

Currents weave, both fierce and calm,
Connecting hearts, unseen.
A silent flow, a soothing balm,
In waters blue and keen.

Miles may stretch and paths divide,
Yet currents bind them tight.
In the waves, their hopes reside,
Love's journey through the night.

Each ripple tells a lover's tale,
Of journeys far and near.
In every surge, in every gale,
Their bond remains sincere.

Horizons wide can't part their ways,
Nor can the roaring sea.
Connected currents guide their days,
In love's sweet melee.

Together through the ebb and flow,
Their spirits finely blend.
No matter where the waters go,
On each other, they depend.

Deep Blue Bonds

Beneath the waves of deep blue seas,
Where silence hums and dreams reside.
There lie the bonds that none can seize,
In oceans vast and wide.

Like anchors dropped in tranquil bays,
Their roots hold fast and true.
Through tempests wild and gentle days,
Together they'll pursue.

Amidst the coral's vibrant hues,
Their stories intertwine.
In every depth, in every muse,
Their hearts forever shine.

With every breath the ocean gives,
Their souls become more strong.
In deep blue bonds, their love lives,
A cherished, endless song.

No wave can break these ties so pure,
No storm can tear apart.
For in the blue, they find the cure,
Of one collective heart.

Sanctuary of Souls

In the quiet of dreams, where whispers roam,
A haven of spirits finds its true home.
Beneath moon's gaze, their secrets unfold,
A sanctuary of souls, stories retold.

Through mist and memory, time gently weaves,
Tales of the past, each soul believes.
Unified hearts, in night's embrace,
Eternal refuge, in this sacred place.

Stars like sentinels above us gleam,
Guiding lost souls through twilight's stream.
Bound by fate, in this ethereal bliss,
A sanctuary of souls, in night's soft kiss.

Here, shadows dance with spectral light,
Cloaked in the mystique of endless night.
Echoes of laughter, sorrow, and song,
Converge in peace, where spirits belong.

In silent reverence, we find our kin,
A realm untouched by mortal sin.
Safe haven for the weary, a cosmic role,
This tranquil realm, our sanctuary of souls.

Hearts in Unison

Beneath the sky where dreams ignite,
Our hearts beat with a fervent light.
In harmony, our spirits rise,
A symphony of boundless ties.

With every step, our paths entwine,
A promise crafted, pure, divine.
Through joy and sorrow, we remain,
Hearts in unison, breaking disdain.

The rhythm of life through veins flows pure,
Together strong, we shall endure.
A melody of love and grace,
Hearts in unison, time can't erase.

In every breath, in every glance,
We find ourselves in sacred dance.
Unified in purpose, bold and wise,
Hearts in unison, touching the skies.

Boundless trust in every stride,
Hand in hand, side by side.
With love's sweet song, our spirits soar,
Hearts in unison, forevermore.

Homestead in Harmony

Where the river bends and willows sigh,
There lies a place where dreams can fly.
A homestead wrapped in nature's song,
In harmony, where we belong.

The rooster's call at break of dawn,
Greets a world where peace is drawn.
Fields of green and skies so blue,
A homestead in harmony, pure and true.

Children's laughter fills the breeze,
Hearts at ease, no need to please.
Under the sun's benevolent ray,
Harmony blooms in everyday.

As twilight whispers tales so old,
Embers glow with warmth untold.
Family gathered round the hearth,
Fleeting moments of simple mirth.

In every corner, love's embrace,
Frames this land, a sacred space.
Forever cherished, eternally,
Our homestead in harmony, wild and free.

Gathering the Kindred

In fields of gold where shadows play,
Kindred spirits find their way.
A gathering beneath the star,
Hearts aligned from near and far.

Through tales of old and laughter shared,
In this circle, all are bared.
Bonds unbreakable, spirits true,
A gathering of the kindred, me and you.

The fire's glow reflects the past,
Memories made and friendships vast.
In unity, our souls align,
Bound by love that's so divine.

Each story told, a thread of light,
Woven through the endless night.
Cherished moments, spirits lift,
Gathering the kindred, our greatest gift.

In silent trust and open hearts,
We come together, never apart.
A timeless bond, a sacred trend,
Gathering the kindred, eternally, friends.

Lunar Lullabies

In the quiet of the night
When the moon begins to rise
Silver beams cascade with light
Across the dark, velvet skies

Whispers grace the evening breeze
Dreams arise from slumber deep
Nature's soothing symphony
Sings the world to gentle sleep

Stars adorn the heavens bright
A cosmic lullaby is spun
Guiding us through realms of night
Until the morning meets the sun

In this twilight, shadows play
Painting visions, soft and sweet
Lunar melodies convey
Serenade where dreams and wishes meet

Every heartbeat, every sigh
Mirrors in the lunar glow
Beneath this canopy so high
Nighttime secrets only moonlight knows

Aquatic Affinity

Ripples dance on crystal bays
Where sunlight kisses waves in play
Whispers of the ocean's praise
Call to hearts both near and far away

Beneath the surface, life exhales
With colors painted rich and fine
Whales serenade with ancient tales
In the depths where waters intertwine

Coral castles, bright and bold
Harbor secrets, old yet new
Every story from waters cold
Tales from seas of tranquil blue

Playful dolphins leap with grace
Ebb and flow in endless rhyme
Through the oceans vast embrace
Time stands still in liquid time

The currents sing their old refrain
Binding hearts to sea's embrace
Aquatic realms where beauty reigns
Our souls find home in endless space

Starry Strands

Caught in the web of a starry night,
Threads of silver, threads of light.
Maps of dreams across the sky,
Starry strands where hopes do fly.

Glimmering paths that weave and twirl,
Mystic dance in cosmic swirl.
Through the vast and dark expanse,
Starry strands, a celestial dance.

Guiding lights in night's embrace,
Shimmering threads in milky lace.
Wishes cast in silent prayer,
Starry strands that fill the air.

Mysteries in each twinkling line,
Ancient tales and signs divine.
Boundless, timeless, uncontained,
Starry strands where souls have trained.

Amidst the strands, we find our place,
Infinite space, eternal grace.
In every glint, a story stands,
Written in those starry strands.

Deep-Rooted Currents

In the depths where shadows play,
Currents deep in vast array.
Roots entwine beneath the waves,
Stories told in silent caves.

Bound by forces strong and wide,
Hidden paths where secrets hide.
In the dark and quiet glint,
Deep-rooted currents leave their print.

Ancient pulses, whispers old,
Mysteries in depths untold.
Flowing through the ocean's face,
A dance of time, in hidden place.

Underneath, a world unseen,
Currents weave a steady sheen.
Past and future intertwined,
Deep-rooted currents, undefined.

In the base where dreams descend,
Silk of oceans without end.
Through their flow, a truth resounds,
In deep-rooted currents, life abounds.

Embracing the Undertow

In the ocean's deep, where shadows grow,
Mysteries whisper, currents flow.
With every wave, the heart does know,
Embrace the undertow, let go.

Beneath the surface, secrets sleep,
The silent void is dark and deep.
Surrender now to waves that sweep,
In losing, treasures you shall keep.

Rip currents pull, with strength untold,
Their fierce embrace, both meek and bold.
Hold tight the helm, but do unfold,
A journey vast, for hearts of gold.

In twilight's hush, horizons fade,
Yet in the dusk, new paths are made.
Through tides and time, the soul is swayed,
Embrace the undertow, unafraid.

For in the dance of ebb and flow,
True freedom lies, in letting go.
With each descent, new worlds to know,
Embrace the undertow, bestow.

Liquid Kinship

In crystal drops, the stories blend,
A liquid bond that knows no end.
Each ripple forms a new dear friend,
In water's arms, our spirits mend.

From mountain peaks to valley's low,
The rivers speak, their wisdom flow.
As one we merge, as one we grow,
A testament to bonds we sow.

In gentle rain, a kinship's voice,
In thunderstorms, a raucous choice.
Together still, we must rejoice,
In water's song, we find our poise.

Across the seas, through every tide,
In liquid form, we all confide.
No distance vast, nor depth can hide,
Our unity, forever tried.

For in the droplets' shining gleam,
We find our strength, we form a team.
Together in this liquid dream,
Our kinship flows, a steady stream.

Inner Compass

Through twilight's whisper, dawn's first light,
A compass guides the heart's true flight.
In shadows deep or open sight,
Its silent touch, a beacon bright.

When crossroads come, and doubts arise,
Look within, beneath the skies.
An inner voice, both wise and wise,
Will lead you past the veiled disguise.

Through storm and calm, it leads the way,
In darkest night or brightest day.
Trust the pull, don't hesitate,
The inner path will never stray.

Beyond the noise, the world's pretence,
A guiding force, transcending sense.
In stillness find your soul's defense,
A north star in the vast expanse.

So follow true, with heart in tow,
Wherever tides of fate may flow.
In every step, you'll come to know,
Your inner compass, let it show.

Streams of Solidarity

Through valleys low and mountains high,
Streams weave their tales beneath the sky.
United in their paths, they try,
To hold each other, by and by.

In every bend, in every turn,
A lesson shared, a truth to learn.
Together in the flow, we yearn,
For solidarity, hearts burn.

From humble springs to mighty rivers,
A strength in unity delivers.
Through every rapid that life shivers,
Solidarity forgives, it quivers.

In times of drought, when hope runs dry,
A stream of kindness will supply.
Together strong, beneath the sky,
In streams of solidarity, we fly.

So join the flow, both you and I,
In currents fierce or calm, we'll try.
With every drop, a bond nearby,
In streams of solidarity, we rely.

Seven Seas of Synchronicity

Across the waves in rhythmic form,
A dance of tides both fierce and warm.
In liquid lines, the worlds align,
A cosmic sign, a grand design.

From shore to shore, harmonics play,
In water's sway, our thoughts convey.
Oceans hum with secrets deep,
In currents' keep, true dreams we seek.

The stars above in mirrored seas,
Reflect a song on tranquil breeze.
Synchronize, unite as one,
Beneath the gaze of rising sun.

Mystic depths of boundless blue,
Reveal the truths within their view.
In every crest and trough we find,
The universe, with hearts aligned.

An ebb, a flow, an endless dance,
In seven seas, fate finds its chance.
Connected through the ocean's call,
We rise, we fall, in unity's thrall.

Linked by Latitude

From north to south, the lines extend,
A global thread where hearts depend.
In every coordinate, we find,
A tethered bond, entwined, aligned.

Longitude may stretch so far,
Yet latitude aligns our star.
Across the globe, in parallels,
Residing where our essence dwells.

Bound by lines we cannot see,
A map of shared reality.
Coordinates in whispered tone,
We navigate, no one alone.

Markers drawn on Earthly sphere,
Yet deeper still, the ties appear.
In regions vast, our spirits roam,
Ever tied to sense of home.

Latitude in measured space,
Defines the steps that we embrace.
In every length and breadth unite,
We journey forth by shared insight.

Fluid Paths

In streams that twist through valleys deep,
Along the grooves, our secrets keep.
Waters glide on fluid paths,
Tracing tales of aftermaths.

From mountaintop to ocean's call,
In every drop, to rivers' thrall.
Meandering through rocks and trees,
With whispered dreams upon the breeze.

Fluid forms that never cease,
In movement find a quiet peace.
Reflecting skies of blue and gray,
In transient flow, we find our way.

Currents shape the lands we tread,
On liquid journeys, paths are spread.
From source to sea, the stories told,
In liquid gold, our fates unrolled.

Pathways drawn in nature's hand,
Frame the life we understand.
In every bend, a chance to grow,
On fluid paths, through ebb and flow.

Swirling Souls

In cosmic dance, our spirits twine,
Swirling through the bounds of time.
A waltz of light, in shadows cast,
Eternal bonds in moments vast.

In galaxy's embrace, we spin,
Our stories woven where stars begin.
In twinkling arcs, our souls ignite,
In swirling paths of endless light.

Through nebulae's resplendent hues,
Our essence mingles, ever fused.
Captivated by the cosmic scrolls,
We find our place as swirling souls.

In constellations' grand ballet,
We twist and turn, we ebb and sway.
In every orbit, hearts are free,
United in the galaxy.

Boundless, timeless, spiraled grace,
Entwined across the vastest space.
With every turn, in whirling whole,
We find ourselves in swirling soul.

Whispers of the Deep

Beneath the waves, the secrets keep,
In ocean's arms, the echoes seep.
The whispers call where shadows creep,
In silent depths, the dreamers sleep.

Coral realms in hues of bright,
Guardians of the briny night.
Mysteries dance just out of sight,
In whispers soft, the heart's delight.

Tales of mermaids, ships long lost,
In waters cold, with pearls embossed.
Ancient myths, the currents glossed,
In whispers, all the memories tossed.

Songs of whales in twilight's grace,
Echoes fill the vast embrace.
A world below, a sacred space,
Whispers weave a tender lace.

From ocean's deep, the stories rise,
In murmurs, truth and beauty lies.
Silent voices, ancient ties,
In whispers, the soul's surprise.

Following the Tide

Golden sands, where dreams reside,
Footprints trace the ocean's stride.
With every wave, we cast aside,
Life's ebb and flow, we follow the tide.

Salt-kissed breezes, whispers light,
Guiding us through day and night.
Journey's end just out of sight,
In tidal dance, we find our flight.

Seashells sing of days gone by,
In each soft wave, a gentle sigh.
Time's rivers flow, and we rely,
On tides to lift our spirits high.

Moon's soft pull, the waters heed,
In rhythm pure, our hearts they lead.
Following tides with silent creed,
In ocean's pulse, our souls are freed.

Each dawn brings a rising wave,
In its swell, our hopes we save.
Following tides, both bold and brave,
We find our path, our spirits rave.

Constellations of Connection

Stars above in cosmic dance,
Bind our souls in wondrous trance.
Across the sky, they take a chance,
In constellations, hearts enhance.

Threads of light weave tales untold,
A map of love, so brave and bold.
In night's embrace, we lose our hold,
In constellations, truth unfolds.

Galaxies far, yet spirits near,
In stardust, dreams appear so clear.
Connections bright, we cherish dear,
In constellations, banish fear.

Mirrored light in lover's gaze,
Reflects the stars' eternal maze.
In boundless sky, our worlds they blaze,
In constellations' warm embrace.

Through space and time, we find our way,
In starlit paths, our hearts convey.
In constellations, love does sway,
Guiding us to break of day.

Swirls of Unity

In colors bright, our spirits blend,
A canvas vast, no start, no end.
Together torn, together mend,
In swirls of unity, hearts transcend.

Brush of fate with strokes so wise,
Creates a world where beauty lies.
Our stories told in vibrant guise,
In swirls of unity, truth applies.

Each shade and hue, a soul's embrace,
In harmony, we find our place.
Unified in love's sweet grace,
In swirls of unity, troubles chase.

Mingled paths in life's grand art,
Connected souls, no space apart.
In every swirl, we're counterpart,
In swirls of unity, one heart.

Through life's palette, we will glide,
In each other's strength, we confide.
Together always, side by side,
In swirls of unity, we abide.

Printed in the USA
CPSIA information can be obtained
at www.ICGtesting.com
LVHW020829030924
789973LV00015B/777

9 789916 863824